Th
of

The Divine Immanence in Nature

by

Henry Thomas Hamblin

Illustrations by Joan Ackroyd
Introduction by Stephanie Sorréll

Science of Thought Press Ltd,
Bosham House, Bosham, Chichester,
West Sussex PO18 8PJ, Great Britian.

Tel/Fax: 01243 572109
email: scienceofthought@mistral.co.uk

First published 1921
10 reprints
Revised edition 2000

© Science of Thought Press Ltd
© Illustrations Joan Ackroyd

Published by:
Science of Thought Press Ltd
Bosham House
Bosham
West Sussex PO18 8PJ
Great Britain

A catalogue record for this book
is available from the British Library.

ISBN 1 903074 03 7

Printed and Bound by RPM Reprographics,
Chichester, West Sussex

Contents

Introduction

The Message of a Flower was first written and published in 1920 and since then it has been reprinted a number of times. This work is important for several reasons; one being that it was Henry Thomas Hamblin's first work after his early retirement from the business world and another being that it conveys so well the gentle and endearing temperament of this unassuming man who, from the founding of the Science of Thought Press, has literally transformed thousands of people's lives throughout the 80 years his work has been known. Although he was a friend and contemporary of Joel Goldsmith, Henry Victor Morgan and Dr Joseph Murphy, he did not want publicity. Instead, he worked quietly and in the background of life in much the same style as the main character in Jean Giono's classic, *The Man who Planted Trees*.

The other reason why this work is of importance today is its reprint comes at a time when our attitudes and responsibility as caretakers of our natural environment have reached critical mass. Although many of us have heard the plea to respect nature for many years now from Rachel Carson's *Silent Spring* to the founding of the Soil Association, Friends of the Earth, Greenpeace and David Attenborough's portrayal of wildlife, we still have a long way to go before we make this connection with nature on a heart level. We know what we should be doing on an intellectual level as we are daily surrounded by scientific proof that unless we change our westernised lifestyles to work *with* the environment, rather than beating it to submission by domination and greed, our environment can no longer support us. This is no longer a crank's viewpoint. It is an irrefutable fact.

I do believe that until we learn to connect to nature on a heart level, rather than a head level, our interconnectedness with nature will always be abstract and idyllic rather than an integrated way of being. Intellectualising nature will always elicit its polar opposite of emotionalism, hence all the emotive rallies that work against faceless organisations that have, through intellectualism, cut off from their feelings. The bridge is the heart; for the heart is the meeting place of mind and feeling.

Again we touch upon the essence of Henry Thomas Hamblin's work and teaching which clearly addresses the heart as something we need to aspire to if we are to understand the meaning of true spirituality. Again and again, the author in his life work states that we need to go beyond the mind, let go of everything we know, and find the heart.

The Message of a Flower, although simple in content, does all of these things. It touches the heart and opens the door to nature. It creates a sense of interconnectedness with nature. As the author shares his experiential contact with the life of flowers and the psychic rapport he found within them, it almost gives the reader permission to do the same.

I am reminded here of the Norwegian philosopher, Arne Naess, who has talked of a new emerging paradigm of 'deep ecology' where experiential and empathic contact with nature can awaken a spiritual awareness of interconnectedness and love for the biosphere in even the most hardened 'hunter'. This viewpoint is rapidly gaining popularity today which only proves that many of us are ready to internalise this message. As true spirituality is experiential, so also is our understanding of nature a spiritual experience.

Stephanie Sorrell
Editor of New Vision
Bosham House
Bosham
Chichester
West Sussex

Let us have constantly before us
a few flowers.
Just a few simple blooms
on our table
or office desk,
to keep us
in touch
with the
infinite.

How It Began

I cannot remember exactly what started me writing. But the first thing I wrote was *The Message of a Flower*. And this is how it came about:

One day, my wife brought in some daffodils and hyacinths, and arranged them in a bowl before me. I looked at them and admired them. They appeared to exert a fascination over me, and I seemed to enter into a new world of beauty, order and perfection, to which they belonged, but to which I had hitherto been a stranger.

So I thought that I would like to write something about them. Sitting down, I wrote what is now the first chapter of *The Message of a Flower*. When it was completed I read it over to my wife, Elizabeth, who approved of it, much to my surprise. Encouraged by this approval I sent the manuscript to a New Thought magazine, *Now*, in San Francisco. Again, much to my surprise, my little article was approved of, and it duly appeared in the little magazine. It was also reproduced in *The Business Philosopher*, a magazine for business men and women, also published in the USA.

Both editors asked for more, so I wrote what now forms chapter two of *The Message of a Flower*. Then, as they asked for yet more, I wrote all the other chapters.

Foreword

The amount of beauty a man sees does not depend upon the abundance of beauty that is around him, for if he is unaware, even though indescribable beauties meet him at every turn, he will see nothing that will either charm his eye, or enrapture his soul. Infinite beauty is all around us — we are immersed in it — but few can see it, for the eyes of their soul are not yet awakened.

Man cannot understand, neither can he see nor recognise, any beauty beyond his standard of discernment. We all believe heaven to be a place of infinite beauty, but if the average man were transplanted there, he would see no more beauty than he does in his present environment, simply because his soul could not appreciate it.

There are beauties around us which we have never yet apprehended. We are blind to them. Yet, when by observation, we learn to appreciate beauties of which we were ignorant before, we find ever before us infinite beauty yet to be discovered and brought into our consciousness; which proves that beauty, being of God, is infinite and, therefore, as the soul awakens, so does the eternal loveliness unfold. This goes to prove that which many metaphysical teachers have said: that beauty is something within the soul, and what man sees about him is a reflection of that which is within him. Therefore the more his soul unfolds and awakens, the more beauty does he see around him. This also tends to show that heaven is not a place, but a state of consciousness, something within the soul. "The Kingdom of God is within you", said Jesus, and studying His teaching one cannot fail to see that what Jesus meant by the Kingdom of God is nothing less than that state of consciousness which we today call 'cosmic consciousness'.

By meditating on the thoughts presented in this little volume, by studying beauty as expressed by simple flowers, we shall not only develop greater appreciation of the loveliness of the divine workmanship, but also enter into a wider consciousness. With this expanded consciousness will come a sense of empathy with every living thing, a realisation of the oneness of all life, and the unity that exists between ourselves and the one complete Whole.

If beauty and
a deep love of
beauty are not
part of your life,
then you have
wandered from
the path of
true achievement.

ONE

The Path of Beauty Leads to God

Gaze at even the humblest flower and you will see in it the loving purposes of God. Before me, as I write, is a bowl of early spring flowers, and as I gaze at them their quiet simple beauty sinks into my soul. They are, to me, messengers from the unseen, beautiful bearers of glad tidings. They tell me in sweet whisperings, things which I could never learn from the harsh life of human endeavour. They speak of love, peace, happiness — they are the visible expression of the eternal loving Good which is behind all and in all. God expresses Himself in an infinity of ways, but in nothing is the divine Purpose more eloquently manifested than in the flowers.

What is the message of the flowers? What are the lessons that they come to teach?

First, they teach that the divine Purpose is the expression of good, therefore God is Good. As I look into the beautiful smiling faces of the flowers before me, they seem softly to whisper: "There is no evil in the divine Plan, only infinite good." As I continue to gaze at their tender loveliness I realise that the Intelligence that produced them cannot be evil, it can be only good. I can apply this to life and affirm this truth by saying; "There is no evil in life's experiences, only infinite good." God being good cannot work evil, neither can He torment me with disease, unhappiness or any lack; all that I suffer now is the result of my own wrong thinking and actions. All is good, and if I will only bring my life into harmony, then it will become, like the flowers, a perfect expression of the loving purposes of God.

These sweet messengers from the unseen tell me that the whole purpose of life and evolution is the greater and ever-increasing expression of good. A flower is guided entirely by instinct and, unconsciously, by the character of the great Intelligence that is behind all natural phenomena. A flower has no "free will", no selfish ambition. It simply expresses the character and love of the infinite Spirit that produces it.

Therefore, when we gaze into a flower we see

the character of God. As I contemplate the tranquil blossoms before me and realise "Who it is" or "What it is" that has brought them into being, can I fear for anything that life can bring me, or have qualms for what the future may hold in store? No! "There is no evil in the divine Intention, only infinite good." That is the message of the flowers.

Secondly, these silent witnesses teach me the lesson of persistence and infinite perseverance. The object of the life of a flower is to beautify the earth, and in dying, to leave behind it the seeds of many more lives of equal beauty. In this object it persists and perseveres, in the face of all obstacles and discouragement. Because a plant has no free will it has nothing to block its expression; driven by instinct it expresses the character of its Creator. Therefore, when I look into a flower, I see again the character of God, which is infinite patience, perseverance and persistence. No matter how unfavourable the soil or climate may be, flowers will attempt to grow and multiply. I remember how, during the First World War, the Allies and Germans turned France into a dust heap of desolation and devastation. As far as the eye could see stretched this awful wasteland of monotonous devastation. Here men lived, month after month, without seeing a tree or a flower, or a blade of grass. It was just mud, shell holes and death.

But Nature was kind even in that place of pitiless horror. Over the torn and rugged earth, over the unlovely marks of men's passion and hatred, gradually began to grow grass and flowering weeds. Plundered Nature was seeking to cover up the nakedness and horror of her wounds, and to show herself once again in all her verdant beauty. Therefore flowers will always persist in growing, no matter how difficult the conditions may be. They do not complain or feel sorry for themselves, neither do they give up in despair— they keep on growing. What wisdom we can learn from the contemplation of a single flower! Infinite persistence, patience and perseverance, these are attributes of the character of God which I see revealed in the blossoms before me.

Thirdly, a flower manifests beauty. This is the natural process, the unalterable object of its life to reflect beauty and loveliness. True, it bears seeds, and blossoms prepare the way for the seeds; but the seeds are produced in order that still more flowers should grow and blossom. The ultimate object is beauty and yet more beauty. When I contemplate the spring blossoms before me, their delicate pure sweetness elicits feelings in my soul too deep to express. Indeed, I have no words with which to clothe the thoughts and feelings that these beauties inspire. They are beyond all human expression, because they are divine. But if I cannot express the emotion that these flowers call into being, yet I can read the message from the unseen which they bear. The message is this: "The Infinite Spirit of Good behind all natural phenomena is a God of beauty. The path of beauty leads to God." When we worship true beauty, we worship the author of true beauty—God. All, that is truly beautiful, is so because it is the expression of the Divine. The flowers say to me: "Be faithful, be true, be earnest, be persistent, be strong and brave, and noble and great. Be all these and more—but do not overlook the cult of the beautiful. "If you forget us," they seem to say, "you forget God. If beauty and a deep love of beauty are not part of your life, then you have wandered from the path of true achievement, you have strayed from the object of your high endeavour."

Man comes into the virgin countryside and cuts and hacks and saws and builds, turning a paradise into a desolation of ugliness and despair. Where once trees and flowers and grasses grew there are now houses and factories. The life-giving oxygen of the natural environment becomes polluted by smoke. Man boastingly exclaims: "It is well, look what I have created! " And angels weeping, say: "Alas, see what he has destroyed!"

Man has free will and can choose good, or he can, instead, create for himself evil. In ignorance, he often chooses the latter, and there is no greater evil than the cult of ugliness for humankind. Ugly surroundings create sickness and unhappiness within the soul of man and ultimately affect the health of the physical and mental body. Cut yourself off from beauty and you cut yourself off from God—from Good. By perpetuating ugliness, man creates evil not just for himself, but his fellow man. It is then sad that man comes into this world, works hard, and then leaves it an uglier world than when he came into it.

What do the flowers say? "Behold us," they whisper, "look upon the purity of our unspoilt beauty and learn the way to God. Look in our faces and you will behold His countenance."

These are the messages from the Unseen which the flowers have brought me. What is their practical application? Can we all plant ourselves in gardens or woods and, like Thoreau, live lives of close communion with Nature? No! We are necessary portions of Life's great Whole, we form part of the great mosaic of the Universe. We dare not neglect our greater responsibilities. Upon us is laid the great task of helping the regeneration of mankind, in winning the emancipation of the soul of man. Therefore, most of us must continue to live in cities and towns of comparative ugliness. Then what can we do?

It is obvious that before we can become happy and healthy we must dispel ugliness from our life and, instead, surround ourselves with only that which is beautiful. All things beautiful are expressions of the Divine, therefore, by surrounding ourselves with beautiful things shall man surround himself with God, and thus gradually take on His image and likeness.

That is in the future. What of the present? Let each of us, as far as possible, bring into his or her life the cult of the beautiful, and dispel ugliness. Let us take responsibility for this by refusing to make or sell ugly things. Let us endeavour to take responsibility for our thoughts. When we see ugly sights let us affirm "the beautiful and true." Let us strive by every means in our power to make this world more beautiful, not for ourselves only, but for all humanity.

Let us have constantly before us a few flowers. Just a few simple blooms on our table or office desk, to keep us in touch with the Infinite. When we are tired or discouraged, let us gaze at these emblems of divine persistence, and take heart again. When we are harassed or flustered, let us commune with these silent messengers from the Unseen, and get in touch with the Infinite which gave them birth. When oppression seems to flourish, let us gaze into these sweet faces and hear again their message of hope; "There is no evil in life's purpose, only infinite good".

It is by thought that we conquer, let the flowers inspire our thought; then will it be beautiful, noble and true; a sure foundation upon which to build the fabric of the future.

When we look lovingly into the tender face
  of a wayside flower,
          we see not
        a mere neglected,
  unappreciated blossom
          wasting its sweetness
        on the desert air,
  but something of the
          imagination
  of the divine Mind.

TWO

The Mind of God

It is now known that natural selection and adaptation to environment form only a very minor part in evolution, and that the changes which take place in animals and plants are due to a dominant idea that exists in the species itself. It is sufficient for the purpose of this booklet to take notice of the fact that modern science is proving what occultists have believed and held for centuries; that manifestation on this plane is the effect of the thought and imagination of a Creative Intelligence. It proves that development and unfoldment are not so much due to environment and selection as they are due to a dynamism, independent of the organic matter. It proves that there is a conscious force, an intelligence, a purpose immanent in everything. If evolution is accepted, we are compelled to admit that all the progressive and complex transformations that have been realised, existed potentially in the primitive elementary form or forms.

We see, therefore, that existing in everything is a creative idea. All that we see is what it is, as the result of the dominant vital dynamism contained within itself. Therefore, when we gaze at a sunset, we do not just see the sunset, but something of the creative Mind. When we look lovingly into the tender face of a wayside flower, we see not a mere neglected, unappreciated blossom wasting its sweetness on the desert air, but something of the imagination of the divine Mind. It is by contemplating and spiritually understanding the beauty within nature that we can enter into the mind and thought and creative imagination of the Divine.

There is an ancient hermetic maxim which runs, "As above, so below"; and if we apply this to our lesson we see something of the wonders of the divine Mind. To most of my readers the creative power of mind is something with which they are familiar. Man is a creator in proportion to his power of creative imagination. First in the unseen, then in the seen; this is the Law of the Universe. First the image is formed in the mind — a vivid picture of what is to be — and it is held there continually until in the outer visible world of matter the thing created begins to manifest. It does not appear all at once or in its complete form. First it takes on its elementary form, and gradually it evolves until the idea is attained and the ambition achieved. A business man creates in his mind a vivid picture of a big and successful business. He holds this image in his mind, and it forms the matrix out of which emerges its replica in the visible world around. First he has a very small business, and although it appears to bear no resemblance to the picture created in his mind, in reality it does. That small business, because it is the creation of that image held in the mind, contains the dynamic urge, the creative idea, which will guide it through stress and challenges into the calmer waters of prosperity, and will cause it to grow and expand until it becomes a replica of the image that has been held persistently in the mind of its creator. Or, again, an inventor forms in his mind the picture of the machine that is to be. He sees it working, and it inspires him by day and fills his dreams by night. Gradually the idea begins to manifest in aluminium and steel and the result is crude and unsatisfactory, but in spite of this there is inherent in it the possible perfected machine that its inventor had visualised. Following many failures and set-backs, the machine is completed and comes into the form that had been originally held in the inventor's mind.

"As above, so below", and the reverse is equally true in this matter, and just as man creates by his picturing and mental imagery, so must it be with the divine Mind. Therefore, what is true of the individual mind must be true of the Universal Mind manifested. That manifestation of loveliness which you hold reverently in your hand is the expression of an image of beauty which has been held in the divine Mind for aeons of time. The flower has not yet evolved to its utmost perfection, for nothing ever reaches perfection, because all is infinite progress and there is no finality. Yet the flawless beauty that we see and the tender sweetness of its loveliness tells me more of the mind of God than all the sermons ever preached.

But in order to understand the mind of God through the contemplation of a flower one must be able to understand a flower spiritually. When we understand spiritually the immaculate beauty of a simple blossom, then perhaps we can understand spiritually the beauty of the divine Mind. As I gaze at a sweet blossom in front of me, I see all the love and tenderness of which it is an emblem, that has been held in the mind of God for countless ages. Before the foundations of the world came into being the beauty of this flower was held in the creative, imaginative mind of God. Moreover, it has been held ever since.

Each morning when I go into our tiny conservatory, which is looked after with loving care by my wife, Elizabeth, I can feel these pure floral brothers and sisters welcoming me with their joyous presence; they touch my heart with their quickening smile. As I stand in their midst I can feel their kind vibrations, their loveliness takes on an ethereal radiance, and I feel that I am indeed in heaven.

I am surrounded by loving smiles and glances, and all these manifestations of the beauty of the divine Mind sink deeply into my soul.

Each flower has its own particular beauty and charm, but they all draw me nearer to the heart of the Divine. It is when I gaze at their unsullied loveliness that I can enter more fully and spiritually into an understanding of the infinite perfection and purity of God. There is no evil in the divine Mind, they tell me. Look upon us, they seem to say, and you will understand that there can be no evil, that there is only infinite Good. There is no disease in the divine Intention, they seem to say. There can be only infinite perfection. And as I gaze at their purity and perfection I get a true spiritual understanding that in God there can be no disease, ill health or any negative thing.

Life need not be the unlovely thing that it is to so many. Its cruelty and ugliness and selfishness are foreign to the divine Idea. Let us study our flowers, and seeing them, learn something of the mind of God, something of the beauty, something of its serenity and deep peace. Let us gaze into the face of a flower and see in it the countenance of God.

We apply this lesson to our own life. If in a flower there is the divine Ideal, gradually finding expression in ever increasing loveliness, then we need to accept that a complementary process of divine unfoldment is taking place within us. This unfoldment gradually seeks expression through an ever-increasing beauty of character and perfection of life. In the divine Imagination is the perfected ideal, the matrix out of which we grow, the model to which our unfoldment is related. Therefore by seeking and yearning after the Divine; by turning constantly in thought and aspiration to the centre of Good, we cannot help but be changed from glory to glory. God is so much more than a blind force finding expression and consciousness in nature and in man. God is not only immanent, He is also transcendent. Words are utterly useless here, for we cannot describe the indescribable, but we can look to God transcendent, guided perhaps by the beauty of a simple flower or a crimson sunset, and find ourselves in the superconscious realm of infinite perfection and radiance. No man has seen God at any time, but the mystic can sometimes catch a fleeting glimpse of the radiance and glory of the Divine.

For those who look upon Nature
with appreciative eyes
and understanding heart,
enter into the inner meaning
of things.
Their thoughts become
spiritualised,
their consciousness enlarged,
their inner life quickened
as the unity of all life
is absorbed into their being.

THREE

The Heart of God

My words are conceived in pleasant places. It is December, and I walk, without hat or coat and in summer clothing, about my garden admiring the few outdoor flowers that are still to be seen at this time of the year. Here in this coastal area of West Sussex we have flowers practically all the year round, and even in the rare event of really cold weather we still have a few blooms in the greenhouse and conservatory.

I am fortunate to have a few of my sweet companions with me all the year round. As I write, a bowl of flowers gaze at me with loving glances, others are in different parts of my room, and near the window is a flowering ice plant with beautiful crimson blossoms bursting out of the tips of its leaves.

My life is indeed blessed; I am surrounded by love, for all the flowers are tokens and manifestations of divine Love. Therefore, as I look at my flowers, love enters my heart and thrills my being, and this love is the love of God.

Flowers are the children of love; they have their origin in the great heart of God. In that great pulsating centre of infinite Love they were born and, being held in the imagination of the divine Spirit, have evolved within the coarse matter of this material world to radiate beauty for the instruction and guidance and inspiration of man.

As I look at their patient loveliness a spiritual understanding comes upon me and streams of divine Love flow into my soul. These pure sweet blossoms act as conductors or telephone wires between earth and heaven, between my fickle heart and the great heart of the Divine.

It has been said that one can only tell what an author really is by his writings. He may in actual life appear ill-tempered and morose, or superficial, or vain, but that is only as he appears to be. What his real inner nature is can only be gauged by his works. This is why great writers are often disappointing; we read their works, and from that form an opinion of their character, yet if we meet them in the flesh we are disappointed because we find somebody quite different from what we expected. This is because their real inner self does not appear on the surface. It is only by their works that you can judge their real character. It is the same with God. God in the abstract, God as He appears in the vast array of books which have been written about Him does not touch our hearts, because such writings do not lead us to the warm heart of the Infinite and its generous all-embracing love. But when we look at a flower and read God's pure sweet message to humanity, we enter into the great divine Heart. As we become conscious of its love and tenderness we are ourselves transformed, as indeed everyone is transformed who contacts this wondrous power.

You ask; "How do you know that the flowers are ministers of divine Love?"

First, I know, because flowers respond to love more than any other thing. Hate or discord in the home will blight or stunt your flowers, but the divine harmony of love will crowd your plants with blossoms. Disharmonious vibrations of discontentment, irritability, selfishness and jealousy will discourage your flowers, and in spite of their best efforts the results will be meagre. But if love and harmony reign in your heart and life and home, if your life is a constant hymn of praise to God, and if your flowers are tended with loving care, then they will respond in a wonderful manner, and vie with one another in their efforts to manifest the infinite Love of God. Yes, flowers respond to love. They bloom much more abundantly and with larger and fairer blossoms if they are tended by the gentle hands of one who loves them dearly. Since my wife has taken over the care of the conservatory the flowers have responded wonderfully to the love bestowed upon them. When the gardener looked after them they were watered and tended to, but there was lacking the love which they now receive. Every shoot is looked at with loving expectation, every little act is a loving ministry, and the flowers respond, for they are the creations of divine Love.

Second, I know the flowers are messengers of love because of what they are. As I gaze at their calm sweet holiness, can I doubt the love of the great Heart in which they had their origin? As I gaze at their enchanting beauty I realise that both their originator and designer is Love. None other could bring forth such pure entrancing workmanship.

To look at the flowers and to enter into their pure messages fills my heart to overflowing, for I realise that love does rule the universe and, consequently, my life. These lovely messengers come straight from the heart of the Creator and tell me that I can trust the One who produced these glorious emblems of perfect love. I can surely trust the Intelligence which created these things, for they tell me that all the motives of the divine are perfect and prompted by love, that God's purposes are always beneficent.

But it is not by simply gazing at the flowers and looking upon them merely as "pretty things" that we can see into, and enter into, the heart of God. Flowers, if we are to read their message, must be understood spiritually. To look at a flower as merely pretty is one thing, but to see a flower as the workmanship of the divine Master Craftsman, and to read in it a message of divine Love, is something entirely different. We need not be poets or artists in order to spiritually understand flowers, for even the most matter-of-fact person can see God's face in a flower if he or she will only look and try to understand.

How then, shall we look in order that we may understand? First of all, we must learn to observe. Let us go up to the flower and examine it carefully and in detail. Notice the exquisite colouring, the delicate texture, the beauty of form, the glorious workmanship. Let these sink into our minds. Now let us notice the simplicity, the purity, the innocence, the expression, and let these sink into our hearts.

Now let us gaze very earnestly at the flower, and try to catch its spiritual vibrations. As we continue to gaze at it we feel its vibrations, being absorbed into our being. The flower changes, it becomes more ethereal, more beautiful, more spiritual, more transparent, it becomes luminous with heavenly light. Let us stand perfectly still and absorb the flower's spiritual beauty and radiance; for we are beginning to see not the physical flower, but its spiritual prototype instead. Now, led by the flower, our thoughts become more spiritual, and we realise that this beautiful ethereal blossom is a thought of God. If this beautiful emblem is a thought of God, what a beautiful mind God has, and if this lovely flower had its origin in God's heart, what a heart of love He must have!

We say of our favourite author or of a noble friend, "That man or that woman has a lovely mind." We say of a poet whose verse draws out the best that is in us, "That man has a lovely soul." We say of a noble person whose life is one of loving service, "That man or woman has a wonderful heart." In like manner, when we realise all the loveliness of a simple flower, and stand dumbfounded before its amazing beauty and understand what the loveliness stands for, what it expresses, we cannot but exclaim, in ecstasy and wonder, "What a wonderful great heart of love God must have to produce these!"

Therefore the message of a flower is one of love. It reveals to us the great heart of God. It disperses all injustices. It tells us that God is not cruel, that the Intelligence which produced this beauty cannot help but be one of infinite love. All our doubts and fears are dispersed and forgotten when we gaze at these dear floral emblems of divine perfection.

Love is always beautiful in its manifestation. It will transform the most ordinary face and make it shine with heavenly light. Some may be plain featured or not generously endowed by Nature, but if divine Love fills their hearts, how attractive they are to those who also belong to the Kingdom of God! We see behind the apparent lack of surface beauty the beauty of the soul and of the character fashioned into the likeness of the Divine.

Humanity, through lack of observation, robs himself of much beauty and enjoyment. So many find the world a dull place, and pass countless beauties by with unobservant eyes. Yet if they would just pause for a few moments; look into flowers and clouds and sunsets, and moon and stars, they would find a wealth of beauty which could never be exhausted in one life or even twenty. They would not only find beauty, but also a message from the Unseen in everything that was admired. For those who look upon Nature with appreciative eyes and understanding heart, enter into the inner meaning of things. Their thoughts becomes spiritualised, their consciousness enlarged, their inner life quickened as the unity of all life is absorbed into the being.

What wisdom we can
learn from the
contemplation of
a simple flower!
Infinite persistence,
patience and perseverance,
these are attributes of
the character of God
which I see revealed
in the blossoms
before me.

FOUR

The Bounty of God

"Consider the lilies of the field,
how they grow;
they toil not, neither do they spin:
and yet I say unto you, That even Solomon
in all his glory was not
arrayed like one of these."

As I look at the flowers before me, clothed in such beauty and elegance that to touch them seems almost a sacrilege, they seem to say; "Oh weary, striving, anxious son of toil, why are you so fearful and troubled ? Look at us and observe our way of life. It is no effort for us to express divine ideas of loveliness and so reveal ourselves before your admiring gaze. We do not strive and struggle, but we simply allow the divine Order to manifest itself through us. We do not express beauty through labour and stress, but we simply are, as we trustfully allow ourselves to be.

"Those of you who are weary and anxious, by contemplating us you can learn from us how to be at peace. We come from a place where there is no stress and care; where everything simply is and where the divine Idea is perfectly expressed. All that we need for our perfect expression is always provided for us by the Father's hand There is no lack or scarcity. If you could learn to trust, even as we trust, then you could also enjoy the bounty of the Father's hand."

Yes, the flowers come to tell us of the inexhaustible bounty of the Divine. Although, outwardly, things may appear very difficult and limited to us, on the inner level, on God's level, there is no limitation or lack. On the human level there are problems, but on God's level there are no problems. God, Who is the source of all supply and abundance, does not withhold His bounty from any who put their trust in Him.

Our willing, our thinking, our striving, our struggling, and our human way of endeavouring to do things, which is quite different from God's way, all these separate us from the Divine so that we are unable to express perfection and harmony like the flowers, but instead disharmony and imperfection. In other words, although the Life of God is harmonious and perfect, we do not express this harmonious perfection but, rather disorder. We create problems of which the flowers are ignorant. The flowers have no problems, simply because they allow themselves "to be", thus allowing the inherent beauty and purpose to become expressed in and through them. Because of this, all that they need for their perfect expression comes to them without effort or strain on their part. They do not have to be anxious for the future; they only have to permit the divine Perfection to unfold.

Is it possible for man to live like a flower? There is a point or ground, Jacob Boehme, the German mystic tells us, behind all our thinking and willing, where we are as God was before Nature began. Is it possible for man to reach, in consciousness, such a point or degree? Yes, for the advanced student. But is there no point that can be reached by the ordinary man and woman? Yes, and the name of it is TRUST !

The flowers, as we gaze at them, or meet them in hedgerow and wood, echo the words of Jesus. They speak, as it were, of their experience. "Look at us," they seem to say, "and see how the Father cares and provides for all who trust Him." Only seek God and put Him first; trust your Father and seek only the

Kingdom of God; do this, and your material needs shall be supplied. This is, briefly, what our lord's message concerning supply is. It all points to the existence of a divine Law, a law which can never fail, a law upon which we can depend, just as we can depend upon the law of gravitation.

This does not mean that we are not to work, or that we are to give up all ambition. It does mean, however, that behind all our efforts and honest strivings there should be a background of trust in God. Behind what we can do ourselves there should be the thought that everything comes from God, and that "except the Lord build the house, they labour in vain that build it". We may sow and we may water, but it is the Lord Who gives the increase. By thinking in this way we bring our life into touch with hidden springs of inexhaustible power; we draw upon secret fountains. We are sustained by That which sustains the whole universe.

Divine bounty and the serene and carefree life are not enjoyed by those who practise, and depend upon greed. Our Lord never taught that we should acquire and hoard, but only that we should lay up treasure in Heaven. In fact, He tells us definitely not to lay up treasure on earth, because of its devastating effect upon the spiritual life—"for where your treasure is, there will your heart be also." If we practise greed then our heart, our soul, our affections, are chained to earth, so that the spiritual life is starved and strangled. As we contemplate the flowers before us we see a beautiful illustration of the carefree life that God would have us live.

The flowers do nothing for gain. They do not manifest their beauty for what they can get out of it, but only to express the divine Idea of beauty of which they are a representative. Man, only too often, robs himself through thinking first of profit and gain, and of expression and service last. If he were to reverse the order and think of his work and service first, and of himself and what he is going to get last, then greater abundance would flow to him. Thinking too much of self-interest robs man not only of the power of expression, but also of true abundance in the things that really are worthwhile.

We need, most of us, to get back to divine Law—to trust God, instead of in purely material sources of supply. We look too much on the seen, and too little upon the unseen sources of supply; we trust too much in material methods, and not enough in the power and resources of Infinite Life. The flowers demonstrate the law which Jesus taught. Cannot we do the same, by putting our whole trust in God?

There are many good people who keep divine bounty away through their attitude of mind. They think that it is not for them and that it is wrong and un-Christlike to be comfortably circumstanced. Consequently, their mind is closed towards divine sources of supply; so that they are at the mercy of the hard ways of the world, in which a few become very rich at the expense of the many, and the weakest become trampled underfoot. Yet God does not want us to be poor and miserable but, rather, He is willing to give us all good and necessary things if we will only ask Him. By turning to God and relying upon Him for supply we make ourselves receptive to divine influences; we open ourselves to receive the inexhaustible provision of God's love.

It is necessary for us to emphasise this point, for many people are worried and harassed about supply and the resources to live decently, who ought not to be so situated at all. The blessings of the spirit are not the only things that God is willing to bestow, for He is just as anxious that we should enjoy temporal blessings also.

Let us, therefore, spread our need out before God, acknowledging that He alone can supply it, and so make ourselves receptive to the abundance that can never fail.

One who enjoys the abundance which comes from God is safeguarded from all the dangers which confront those who win prosperity in other ways; that is, those ways from which God is excluded. If we leave God out of our calculations we may become very successful in life, but our success and prosperity will have a deadening effect upon our soul. We may become not only self-satisfied, but we may even become superior, looking down upon our fellows who are less successful than ourselves as slightly inferior creatures, whereas they most probably are our superiors in character and all that matters most to the soul.

But one who relies upon God for supply never becomes puffed up with pride, for he knows that it all comes from the Lord and that he depends upon divine sources completely. Therefore, there is no room for pride or self satisfaction, but only an opening for humility and gratitude.

Again, one who relies upon divine supply is saved from a lack of refinement. Like the flowers, he is always in the best of taste. There is none if little coarseness in his nature. Neither is there a tendency for extravagance. He is not guilty of indulging in expensive luxuries, while thousands are starving. Like the flowers, he is content with sufficient for his perfect expression, and therefore he gives the balance to the work of the Lord, the spreading of Truth, through which the Kingdom of God is extended on earth.

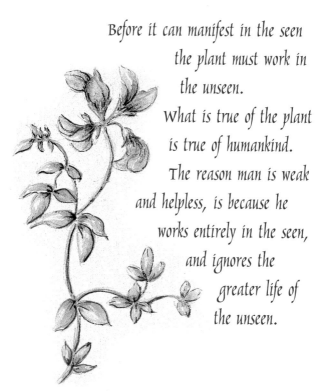

Before it can manifest in the seen
the plant must work in
the unseen.
What is true of the plant
is true of humankind.
The reason man is weak
and helpless, is because he
works entirely in the seen,
and ignores the
greater life of
the unseen.

FIVE

From the Unseen to the Seen

A flower receives direct from the Creator's hand all that it needs for its perfect unfoldment. The gentle rains feed it and wash it, and when the skies are clear it is refreshed by the dew. It lives a life of true opulence; in the early morning it is covered with diamonds, each drop of dew a shining sphere, a miniature sun, a faithful representative of the Light which proceeds from the Divine. God in the flower. God in the dewdrop.

The flower receives all that it needs. In the soil in which it grows are contained all the substances, other than light and air and water, that it needs. Many subtle chemicals are hidden in the soil, the Earth Mother providing her children with all the nourishment that they need.

As the gentle rain falls from the sky, and sinks into the earth it sets free the nourishment for the hungry roots. The environment is provided out of which the flower can manufacture its own beauty. Its beauty does not fall upon it from the sky. The flower has to evolve from within. The flower's success in expressing beauty does not come from without, but from within. Its life is one of constant activity. From the time the seed is put in the ground onwards the little plant is struggling and striving, but without strain or worry, ever seeking to express itself more perfectly. The substances which are set free from the soil by the rain, the dew and the light and the air, would all be futile if the plant did not make use of them. Perfection does not come without application; it can only be attained through persistence and perseverance.

The effort and application of a flower are, however, very different from the labour and joyless strivings of man. It is a joy to express the inherent divine Perfection, and wonderfully rewarding to grow and show forth beauty and loveliness. The effort is without strain, worry, or anxiety; it is just as joyful as the playfulness of a kitten in the sun. It is as if the flower is saying; "Oh weary hearted man, can you not make your work also a joyous, light hearted expression of the Divine?"

Again, the beauty which we see expressed above the ground is the effect of something which has taken place underground. If it were not for the hidden root, and the work which the root does, there could be no blossom, no leaf, no beauty. The flower depends upon its root more than upon anything. Its delicate fibres are constantly spreading and searching for nourishment from the Earth Mother. Before it can manifest in the seen the plant must work in the unseen. The more vigorously it works underneath the ground, the greater will be the growth above the ground. The amount of beauty that a flower manifests, together with the vigour of its growth, are the measure of its work in the unseen. But for the work underneath the ground there could be no strength of stalk or leaf, no beautiful blossom to cheer and enrich our lives. What is true of the plant is true of every son of man. The reason man is so weak and helpless, and his life so barren of beauty and true achievement, is because he works entirely in the seen, and ignores the greater life of the Unseen. Man is constantly striving in the world of effect and neglects the greater world of cause. Largely, mankind lives entirely the objective life of the senses. By the materialistic nature of our thoughts we cut ourselves off from our invisible divine spiritual source. Therefore his life is poor and impoverished like a plant that is starved of vital minerals. Although man prides himself on his intellect, yet he pollutes nature wherever he goes. Instead of the fairy glen, filled with indescribable beauties and enchantments, the singing birds, the trees, flowers, grasses and sweet odours, man has built ugly concrete buildings and high-rise flats which by their soulless nature are an oppressive influence on those who live in them.

"Oh! for a change from the alley drear,
To the shores where the surges sweep,
And the breath of heaven comes softly in,
From the wastes of the mighty deep."

Jesus wept over Jerusalem, and if He were here today He would find tears enough to shed over the places in the world where people still live in poverty and slums. This is largely the work of vanity, greed and intellectual arrogance. This disfigurement of the earth is the work of man, divorced from God, by his own disharmonious thoughts and beliefs. This is the result of living the life of the senses and ignoring the inner life of the spirit, of relying on the evidence of the senses instead of listening to the inward voice of the spirit. Man is like a plant whose roots are defective and which cannot therefore bring forth blossoms, for it does not draw from the earth the nourishment that it needs. Man does not work in the Unseen, therefore he cannot accomplish anything worth while in the seen. His life is stunted, dwarfed, and lacks true achievement, because his inner life is neglected and ignored. It produces ugliness and destruction, instead of beauty and harmonious development. In the inward life of the spirit is the source and course of all beauty of expression, all lofty achievement, all true success in the outward life of the senses. Yet, within himself alone man can discover the energy, wisdom and inspiration that can make his life sublime. It is only from within that man can draw upon inexhaustible powers for the achievement of lofty ideals and the rendering of highest service.

Consider for a moment the life of the average man who neglects the inward source of power.

Firstly, he lacks wisdom.

Instead of being guided in Truth, and led onto

the path of spiritual attainment, he blunders on in blindness and ignorance. Not realising that things are not what they seem, and that the evidence of the senses can be so misleading as to be generally almost the exact opposite of Truth, he continually acts in a way that brings unhappiness into his life. He seems to be plagued by negative influences from which he cannot escape. He thinks that by making money he can become happy, and then finds to his dismay that when he has made money, happiness is more elusive than ever. If he becomes successful in one thing he fails lamentably in another. As soon as he overcomes one obstacle another appears. For instance, he may climb from poverty to wealth and then have his home filled with discord or illness. Life then becomes a succession of expensive operations, consultations with learned specialists, hiring of trained nurses; it is full of anxiety and care. He then realises that a poor man with a healthy wife and family is better off than himself. Blindly, he stumbles on, never seeming to be able to rid his life of negative conditions but, instead, only meeting its changed form in another debilitating set of circumstances. When faced by the many problems of life he has nowhere to turn for guidance and direction. He has no inward conviction telling him which way to go. Instead, he has to depend on his own finite understanding, the evidence of his senses, the experiences of other people; therefore he comes, in every case, to a wrong decision.

Secondly, he lacks inspiration.

All inspiration comes from within. It springs from within the superconscious mind, yet it fails to manifest in those who live entirely the objective life of the senses. All men and women of great achievement have made a point of setting aside time to be alone, in order to obtain inspiration from within. Although they were probably not conversant with the laws of which they were making use, instinctively they sat in the silence to meditate and reflect, and drew from their superconscious mind the inspiration that they needed. But the average person thinks that he can do without that which the greatest have always found necessary and, consequently, lives their life entirely in the senses, and with disastrous results. No wonder man's life lacks inspiration and true achievement. No wonder his highest efforts fail to find an echo in other hearts; no wonder he is neglected by the world; for one who is not himself inspired can never arouse enthusiasm in others. He wonders why, in spite of all his striving, his work is mediocre, so lacking in the divine quality of originality.

Thirdly, he lacks power.

By the disharmonious nature of his thoughts man separates himself from his divine Source. He relies upon his feeble finite powers instead of connecting himself with the Source of the universe. Therefore, all that he does is accomplished by huge effort and painful striving, and when he has done all, it is hardly worth the effort. The only achievements in world history that have been worth doing, and which have endured have been the result of spiritual insight and inspiration. Here, spiritual achievement has remained long after its originator has passed on. And these lofty ideals are born of the spirit, they spring from the superconscious mind; they are the fruit of divine inspiration.

No wonder man's life is ugly and depressed; he cuts himself off from his root life, from his divine Source of all power, inspiration and wisdom. Before man can achieve something really worth while he must do as the flowers do, work in the Unseen and there draw upon infinite supplies. Just as the beauty of a flower depends upon its root growth, so does man's life and achievement depend upon the work that he does in the silence.

Within every flower is hidden the divine Ideal – there is within it an urge, which makes it ever strive after a more perfect expression. Within man is hidden the same divine Ideal, the infinite Perfection striving to find expression in his life; but unless he listens in the silence of reflection and meditation, he cannot access wisdom or become conscious of the Divine in order to align his ideals with it. He remains lifeless and uninspired.

"Seek first the Kingdom and all these things shall be added unto you", said Jesus, and His words are as true in these days of complicated finance as they were in the simpler days when He preached on the shores of the Galilean Sea. The amount of true success that we can demonstrate in our outward life is directly proportional to the amount of time that we devote to the spiritual inner life. When man finds his inner centre, he discovers that he has true creative power, and what he creates in the unseen becomes manifest in the seen. The development of creative power demands very earnest effort. The building up in the mind of the ideal, the self that is to be, demands mental activity, perseverance and concentration, but these are well repaid, for those who accomplish in the Unseen, succeed in life without apparent effort, can afford to hold success very lightly, and therefore are not the slaves of their own success.

Great leaders of industry, men and women of imagination and vision who guide the affairs of nations, may not be given to prayer or entering the silence as we know it, but, unconsciously they practise what amounts to the same thing. They spend time alone and think in undisturbed quietness, and when they have exhausted all the resources of objective thinking, they dismiss the matter and rely upon inspiration. This is very similar to the Christian casting his care upon the Lord and relying on God for an answer. They both rely upon the superconscious mind, which is in touch with the universal Intelligence, to find an answer to problems which the objective mind can never solve.

The roots of a flower are always at work, continually drawing nourishment from the earth, which it transmutes into beauty and loveliness. In the same way man can, by meditation and real prayer, so train his inner mind that, in time, it constantly draws upon its divine Source and brings the power of the Infinite into expression. Then, and only then, does his life manifest beauty instead of ugliness, love instead of hate, harmony instead of discord.

Within every flower is hidden
the divine Ideal,
there is within it
an urge,
which ever makes
it strive after
a more
perfect expression.

SIX

The Pursuit of an Ideal

The quest of an ideal is the main object of the life of a flower. It seeks continuously to express, ever more faithfully, the divine Ideal that is hidden within. Conceived in the great mind of the Creator is the perfect ideal flower, and there is in the plant a divine urge seeking ever to give more complete expression to this perfect idea. Therefore, when we gaze at a flower we see, not merely "a pretty thing", but a perfect ideal born in the mind of God countless aeons ago, and still quietly pressing forward to find expression in ever increasing loveliness.

The same process is going on in man. There is in him the divine urge which calls him to ceaseless effort and striving, to manifest in his life the divine human being which is imaged in the mind of his Creator. "Be ye therefore perfect even as your Father in Heaven is perfect", said Jesus, and this is the grand ideal which all mankind, if it is to fulfil its glorious destiny, must ultimately seek after and strive to attain to.

Flowers go patiently on, living their countless lives through the ages, ever passing on to greater loveliness. They have no choice between good and evil, they have not to learn, through painful experience, the error of their ways. They pass steadily on to their goal, ever in the path of their destiny. But man has a far more glorious destiny, he is marching on to godhood. "Be ye perfect" is the divine injunction of the greatest divine Teacher of the ages. This is the voice of the Christ, the Perfect One, cherished in the heart of the Father. We are gods in the making whose aim is perfection, this is the glorious meaning of life to those whose eyes are blessed with true vision and whose soul has perceived this great revelation. But man goes astray; for although he feels within him the dynamic urge, he misunderstands its message. He yearns after better things, but thinks that he can find happiness and satisfaction through the material life and sexuality. But he finds he is merely chasing a will-o-the-wisp; for he only encounters disenchantment, sorrow, disappointment and despair. The lure of materialism, the fallacy of possession, the greed for power lead him relentlessly on to unhappiness and disappointment.

But the awakened soul hears the voice of true wisdom. He sees the attractions and enchantments of the world but does not become enslaved by them. Instead, he sees them all in the light of Eternity. "Be ye perfect even as your Heavenly Father is perfect," sounds continuously in his soul. To him, the glamour of the world, the lure of fame and power, are transitory and only lead to disappointment. Such a one is walking the path of his destiny in full consciousness. He hears the voice of his soul calling him to higher and better things. Like the flower, he responds to the call of the great Ideal; he ever presses forward to express in his life and character some of the vision he has seen.

One of the greatest truths that can come to man is this: that when he holds an ideal before his mental vision, no matter how misty that ideal may be, he immediately invokes the divine Power within him into expression. The truly great men of all ages have been those who have followed the Light; who have pursued a great ideal. No one who was not inspired has ever been able to accomplish anything really worthwhile, for it is only through idealism that the divine inward Power can be brought forth into expression.

A flower does not express ugliness, for even the humblest blossom is beautiful. It may not compare favourably with its more extravagantly arrayed or more ethereal brothers and sisters, but it is really beautiful. The plain flowers, if I may use such a term, always appeal to me, for they strive so hard to do the best they can, to express what to them is their highest ideal of beauty. The simplest and most common flower, if any flower can be described in this way, if examined in the right spirit, is beautiful, indeed it is a wonderful piece of exquisite craftmanship. We never see a flower come out into blossoms that are bloated and coarsened by indulgence, neither do we see petals that are distorted by passion. No matter how homely the flower may be it possesses a certain inherent purity, as if making an honest attempt to 'be the best it can'. But the faces of men are only too often marred by excess and disfigured by passion. When man ceases to strive after the divine Ideal, when he leaves off climbing after higher and better things, when he ceases to seek the highest aspirations of the soul, he is led aside into a wilderness, only to find himself a captive in the castle of despair. Christ said, "I am the door. He that entereth not by the door into the sheepfold but climbeth up some other way is a thief and a robber." When man tries to find happiness and to satisfy the divine urge by sensual means, instead of pursuing the pure and beautiful, the Christ Ideal which is implanted in every man, he rapidly falls into chaos. When man pursues the highest and best, he produces constructive action and "all the divine Forces hasten to minister to his eternal joy", to aid him in his upward climb. But when he ceases to strive after a high ideal, all his efforts produce destructive action and his life begins to disintegrate and fall apart. This is so often reflected in the faces of our human brethren.

The flower ever strives after a bright ideal. From the time the seed begins to sprout to the end of its days the plant seeks to manifest its beauty and to radiate the Creator's Love. "Look at us," they cry, "and see in our beauty the evidence of God's loving kindness. Behold ! He sends us to minister by our beauty to your joy and pleasure. Look at us! And learn a lesson from our ceaseless yet joyful activity. Every day and every minute do we express the highest and best that is within us, that we may demonstrate by our loveliness and sweet fragrance the surpassing love of God." Yes, the flower ever strives to make the world more beautiful, it endeavours to uplift the sad hearts of humankind.

A flower not only starts life cherishing a bright ideal, it always continues to do so. It never regresses, it never lets its ideals become dimmed. Often man starts out on life inspired by lofty ideals and energised by yearnings after better things. As he experiences the divine urge within, he determines to follow the Light, to hitch his wagon to a star. And all goes well for a time, but the pursuit of wealth, the hustle and bustle of city life, the low aims of the bulk of mankind, gradually dim the bright image, until at last, one after another, his ideals are relinquished. When this takes place it is goodbye to all true achievement, farewell to all real progress. The inward Power lies dormant, for it is only the pursuit of high ideals that can bring it into expression. Those of my readers who have lost their ideals should take a lesson from the flower.....

The flower never ceases to follow the highest and best, and you too must go back to the place where you parted from your ideals, and find them again. It is only by doing this that your life can become a true and lovely success, and travel the path of destiny. It is only by so doing that you can arouse the divine Power within your soul and bring it into expression. You must find again your lost ideals, and brush away the dust of disappointed years, learning again to follow the light, to press upward to the highest and the best.

This is the only path to real success, this striving after the highest and truest aspirations of the soul. What are health, wealth and love compared with high achievement, ambitions realised, the unfoldment of the soul, the fruits of the Spirit, the development of a Christlike character, the attainment of God consciousness? Seek first the Kingdom and all these things shall be added unto you. Those who seek the highest and best find the Kingdom, and by their discovery they enter into all things. Seek the highest and best, be animated by noble ambitions, and find the Christ within the soul, and you can no more lack than an angel in Heaven.

Blessings both spiritual and temporal come to the one who has entered into the fold, he goes in and out and finds pasture. He does not have to think about his health. Neither does he have to think about evil or danger, for; "no evil can come nigh. .. nothing can hurt or destroy".

Many are deterred from following the highest and best, because they are assured that it does not pay. But believe me it is the only life that does pay. Does it pay an artist to paint "pot boilers"? Never. There has never been a "pot boiler" yet that has not done irreparable damage to its perpetrator's reputation. And yet the majority of people go through life producing, to their shame and ruin, nothing but "pot boilers". For the sake of a mere weekly wage, for a paltry business, for fear of what people might say or think, they give up their ideals, they cease to follow the Light. And yet there is a life of surpassing loveliness, of ineffable joy, of truest success, which might be theirs if they would only follow the best that is in them.

Men and women, which shall it be?

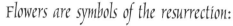

Flowers are symbols of the resurrection:
The silvery whisper again
comes from the flowers
before me:
'We bring you tidings
that all is well.
Your loved ones are safe
in the great
heart of
divine Love.'

SEVEN

Easter Glory

The previous chapters have been read by my wife, Elizabeth, who tells me that I have left out the most important message of all, namely, that flowers are symbols of the resurrection. She is thinking of that grave a mile away, where little Dick, our ten year old son is buried and with him so many of her earthly hopes—and mine.

Ah me, life would be sad and hopeless indeed, if our faith did not stretch out firm hands beyond the grave—if it could not tell us that all is well. But the flowers greet us with loving and sympathetic glances: they would gently chide us for our sorrow, saying: "Dear mortals, try not to be sorrowful this day, because of those who have passed from your sight, but not from your company. We bring you messages of hope, for we come from the country of eternal day. We are messengers from that Love that will never forsake you — that can never let you go."

Yes! Yes! Love that will never let us go.

How soon we forget that wonderful Love, past all understanding, and beyond all definition. I am reminded of Dr. Pulsford's words in Quiet Hours:

"What God takes from us, returns to us in another way. He gives back to us our friends more deeply, more tenderly, more sacredly, after they have been taken from us by death. When they become wholly His, they become more intimately ours. The intimacy before death pertains more to the flesh and its senses: after death it pertains more to the spirit and its inner affections. It is as though God gave them to us, out of His own heart, with the holiness and fragrance of the divine Nature added to them. By death they become too chaste, too heavenly, for our light moods and our common hours; they visit us only in our holiest moments. They act upon us, therefore, as motives to prayer, watchfulness, and retirement of spirit. They greatly befriend our best interests. As the Lord before His death was 'with' His friends, but afterwards 'in' them, so our holiest friends help us the more, when they put off flesh, and are no more seen."

The silvery whisper emanates again from the flowers before me: "We bring you tidings that all is well. Your loved ones are safe in the great heart of divine Love. They are His loved ones whom He delighteth to honour. The Lord of Love is coming again and will swallow up mortality in immortality and corruption in incorruptibility. Then your loved ones will appear again in objective life, raised in glory with Him."

Ah yes! Blessed thoughts, "For this was the purpose of Christ's dying and coming to life — namely that He might be Lord both of the dead and the living" (Romans 14. 9.)

And so the gracious flowers remind us, whenever we glance at them, of the victorious coming again of our Lord — of that glorious Easter when all the precious fruits of the divine Harvest shall be gathered in; when Christ shall reap where He has sown. He sowed in pain, sorrow and apparent defeat. He shall reap in joy, glory and overwhelming victory.

Take heart, readers. Behind imperfection is the divine Perfection. Behind the gloom the sun is shining. Behind all sorrow is the Eternal Joy. Let us enter into the heart of things and realise this glorious truth now. For we can do so. We can pierce the gloom and see the glory behind it all. We can enter the inner Holy of Holies now. We can realise in our soul that all is indeed well. How? By looking for God in Nature. By looking for God in our fellow creatures. By looking for God in all the experiences of life. By communing with God in the Secret Place. By praising God and being in a state of gratitude every hour of the day. Often the reason for not being filled with joy is because we do not praise and thank God sufficiently. Constant praise and thanksgiving brings happiness to the heart and joy to the soul. Therefore, let us look at the flowers which God has given us and thank Him for the truth that all is well.

Unfolding, like a rose

The life of attainment, or of regeneration, is not an easy one. Nothing that is worth achieving is easy. For instance, it is not easy to become a first class musician, or artist, or mathematician. Yet, if a student goes about his task in a right way, his course of study becomes a harmonious progression. Stage by stage he moves upwards and onwards. As soon as he has mastered one stage, he moves on to a more difficult one; until at last he finds himself a master musician, or artist, or mathematician, as the case may be.

It is the same with the life of attainment. If we go about it in the right way, then our progress is like the unfoldment of a flower. The unfoldment of a rosebud, for instance, is a most wonderful and complicated process. And yet, although it is such a complicated and seemingly impossible task for the rosebud, it does not worry about it, and does not find it difficult. It does not find it difficult, because it does not resist the work of the creative Genius within it. There is an idea of a perfect rose within the bud, which also is held forever in the Mind of God. This perfect idea finds harmonious expression because the rosebud does not resist it. If the rosebud were able to think, and if it were to say to itself: "I am a perfect bud," or if it were to affirm: "I am God's perfect rose", and still be determined to remain unaltered and undeveloped, then it would be resisting the changes which unfoldment brings, and trouble and difficulty would be the result.

A moment ago, I said the life of regeneration is not an easy one. It is, however, no more difficult than the unfolding of a flower. It is just as harmonious and orderly, and even more God-directed. Within the unfoldment of a flower we see natural law unfolding divinely created ideas. Within our own unfoldment we are each one of us directly and intimately connected with and helped by the Holy Spirit. But, all the same, our spiritual unfoldment is just as harmonious and orderly as the unfoldment of a flower, and follows similar laws, for there is a natural law in the spiritual realm.

Other titles by the Author

The Little Book of Right Thinking	ISBN 1-903074-00-2
My Search for Truth	ISBN 0-9531597-7-9
The Story of my Life	ISBN 0-9531597-8-7
Within You is the Power	ISBN 0-9531597-2-8
The Power of Thought	ISBN 1-903074-02-9
Life Without Strain	ISBN 0-9531597-9-5
Divine Adjustment	ISBN 0-9531597-6-0
The Open Door	ISBN 0-9531597-3-6
Life of the Spirit	ISBN 0-9531597-4-4
His Wisdom Guiding	ISBN 1-903074-01-0
The Hamblin Book of Daily Readings	ISBN 0-9531597-5-2

Also recommended:

The River That Knows The way
Edited by Stephanie Sorréll
ISBN 0-9531597-0-1

The Inner Temple by Hanne Jahr
ISBN 0-9531597-1-X

New Vision – a bi-monthly magazine
(formerly *Science of Thought Review*)
founded by Henry Thomas Hamblin

for further information contact the publisher:
Science of Thought Press Ltd.
Bosham House, Bosham, Chichester,
West Sussex PO18 8PJ, England

Telephone/Fax: +44 (0) 1243 572109
Email: scienceofthought@mistral.co.uk